Life in the Temperate Grasslands

Life in the Temperate Grasslands

Laurie Peach Toupin

Watts LIBRARY™

Franklin Watts
A Division of Scholastic Inc.
New York • Toronto • London • Auckland • Sydney
Mexico City • New Delhi • Hong Kong
Danbury, Connecticut

To my mom and dad,
who loved me enough to let me follow my dream

Note to readers: Definitions for words in **bold** can be found in the Glossary at the back of this book.

Photographs © 2005: Corbis Images: 10 (Tom Bean), 50 (Bettmann), 40 (Tom Brakefield), 29 (W. Perry Conway), 18, 52 (Raymond Gehman), cover (Robert Holmes), 45 (Jeff Vanuga); NHPA/Rich Kirchner: 31; Photo Researchers, NY: 5 right, 48, 49 (Charles V. Angelo), 38 (Toni Angermayer), 27 (Mark Boulton), 21 left (Geoff Bryant), 22 (Nigel Cattlin), 41 (S.L. & J.T. Collins), 37, 39 bottom (Tim Davis), 33 (E.R. Degginger), 42 (Jim Grace), 11 (Gilbert S. Grant), 14 (JVZ/SPL), 6 (C.K. Lorenz), 5 left, 36, 39 top (Maslowski), 34 (Tom McHugh), 2, 21 right (Jim Steinberg), 23 (I.J. Strange); Courtesy of Richard Peach: 24; Superstock, Inc./Charles Marden Fitch: 32; Visuals Unlimited: 16 (Wally Eberhart), 12 (Richard Thom).

Illustration p.9 by Bob Italiano

The photograph on the cover shows the Manitoba Prairie. The photograph opposite the title page shows the Konza Prairie Research Natural Area in Kansas.

Library of Congress Cataloging-in-Publication Data

Life in the temperate grasslands / Laurie Peach Toupin.— 1st ed.
    p. cm. — (Biomes and habitats)
Includes bibliographical references (p.   ).
ISBN 0-531-12385-5 (lib. bdg.)
1. Grassland ecology—Juvenile literature. I. Title. II. Series.
QH541.5.P7T68 2005
577.4—dc22

2004013282

Contents

The name "prairie chicken" aptly describes this grassland grouse. It lives on the prairies of North America and is about the size of a small chicken. Its mating rituals inspired the dances of the Plains Indians.

Chapter One

No Trees, No Problem

At 6:30 a.m. one day in April, sixty-five excited spectators gather in Karlos and Elaine Kaelke's barn in Lockwood, Missouri. Everyone holds binoculars and wears a warm jacket. No one speaks, but all peer intently across a farm field just beginning to show signs of spring.

Soon, about twenty-five brown and white greater prairie chickens come into view. The birds strut, jump, and "boom" as they vie for the attention of a female.

The males boom by expanding the bright orange sacs located at the base of their beak. The louder and more impressive the sound, the more likely they are to attract a mate.

"This is what we came to see!" someone whispers excitedly. These birds were once the main attraction at Kaelke's Prairie Chicken Bed & Breakfast, which sat on a prairie chicken "booming ground."

Every April, Karlos and Elaine opened their home to visitors who came from all over the United States to watch the ancient prairie chicken mating ritual. However, the number of chickens who used the booming ground slowly dwindled.

In 1997, only one male showed up. "It was a sad sight," Karlos says. "A very lonely picture." The Prairie Chicken Bed & Breakfast closed its doors.

The disappearance of the Kaelkes' prairie chickens reflects what has happened to much of the temperate grasslands everywhere.

All Over the World

At the heart of every continent except Antarctica lies grassland—a vast, wide-open, treeless space where nothing grows taller than the tallest blade of grass. Harsh weather conditions, grazing animals, and fires keep trees and woody shrubs from growing in these areas.

Precipitation ranges from 10 to 30 inches (25 to 75 centimeters) a year. Any less, and these areas would become desert. Any more, and they would turn into forest.

Tropical Versus Temperate

There are two types of grasslands—tropical and temperate. Each occurs within certain latitude bands. Tropical grasslands grow near the equator—between the Tropic of Cancer and the Tropic of Capricorn. These grasslands include the savannas of Africa and South America. Temperate grasslands grow in latitude bands above and below the Tropic of Cancer and the Tropic of Capricorn. Each of these grasslands is considered a **biome**, a large community of organisms living in an area that is defined largely by climate.

Tropical and temperate grasslands together once covered more than 40 percent of the world's land surface. Today, a little more than 25 percent, or one-quarter, of the surface of

The world is made up of biomes. Look on the map and find out which biome you live in.

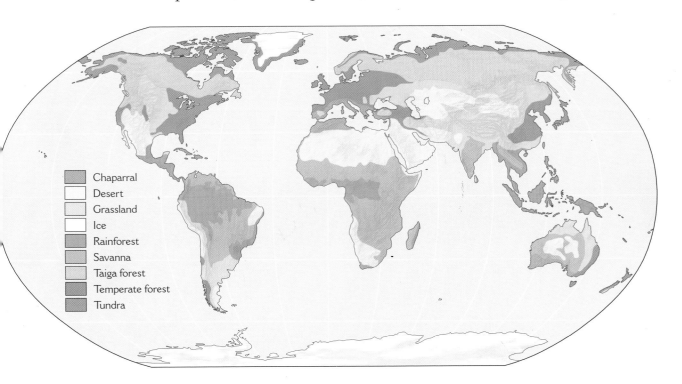

Chaparral
Desert
Grassland
Ice
Rainforest
Savanna
Taiga forest
Temperate forest
Tundra

Earth is grassland. Much of this decrease was the result of the invention of the steel plow by John Deere in 1837.

Grass plants develop a thick network of roots. This root system retains moisture and nutrients during droughts, fire, or cold, allowing grasses to grow in the worst of conditions. Dirt that is meshed with roots doesn't blow away. Instead, it builds up year after year, making grasslands home to some of the most fertile soils on the planet.

But this same root system made it impossible for the early American settlers to farm the prairies. The cast iron plow, made for looser forest soils in the East, couldn't cut through

Grass Building Blocks

Early settlers used Buffalo grass to build **sod** houses, called soddies. These small structures had walls built of stacked layers of uniformly cut turf. The sod "bricks" contained such a thick network of roots that they held together without any cement or mortar.

the thick soil of the Midwest. The steel plow could, however. Once people had a way to cut through the layers of tangled plant roots, it wasn't long before farmers turned acres upon acres of temperate grasslands into plowed fields for crops. This reduction of native grassland has caused a decline in the wildlife that lives in this biome, such as the prairie chicken.

A Grassland by Any Other Name

In North America, grassland is called the prairie. In South America, it is called the pampa. In southern Africa, grassland is called the veldt, and in Europe and Asia, it is known as the steppe. All of these names mean the same thing: vast areas of land with no trees and lots of grass.

Get Along, Little Doggy

When Americans hear the word *prairie*, visions of the Great Plains with grasses as tall as small trees come to mind. This is the tallgrass prairie, where plant height averages 4 to 8 feet (120 to 240 cm). Big bluestem grass grows tall enough to hide a person on horseback. But there are three types of prairies in this country. Each is named according to the height of the grass that grows there: tall, medium, and short.

Medium grass prairies do not receive as much rainfall as tall grass areas. Grasses range from 2 to 4 feet (60 to 120 cm) in height and include Little Bluestem, wild ryes, and fescues.

Short grass prairies receive the least amount of rainfall. The tallest grass plant on short grass prairies may grow 18

Little bluestem is a common medium grass prairie plant. Small birds depend on its seed in the winter.

Buffalo grass is known for its high tolerance for long droughts and extreme temperatures.

inches (45 cm). Buffalograss, which supported the great herds of bison, is common.

South American Cowboys

The word *pampa* comes from Quechua, the language spoken by the Incas, native people of South America, and means "flat surface." The pampa covers an area of more than 290,000 square miles (751,000 square kilometers), flowing across Argentina from the Atlantic Ocean to the Andes Mountains on the west coast of South America. The western pampa verges on desert because so little rain falls. The eastern pampa, however, is considered one of the best grazing lands in the world for cows, goats, and sheep. This land is the center of Argentina's agriculture and home of the gaucho, the South American cowboy. The predominant plant, pampa grass, can grow to be up to 9 feet (270 cm) tall.

Africa's Sweet and Sour Grass

The word *veldt* means "field" in Afrikaans, one of the languages spoken in South Africa. The name refers to the grassland located in South Africa and Zimbabwe. Farmers divide the veldt into "sweet" and "sour." The sweet veldt is in the west, where less rain falls. The native red grass is sparse but good for cows to eat all year long. More rain falls in the east and grass is more abundant, but it is nutritious only in the summer, and harmful, or "sour," to the cattle the rest of the year.

Really Big

The steppe extends some 5,000 miles (8,000 km) across Europe and Asia. It begins in Ukraine and flows eastward through Russia and Mongolia. The steppe is the world's largest temperate grassland. The area is known for its scorching summers and freezing winters. Annual precipitation is not

Black Gold

The rich, deep soil of the prairie was formed after the last ice age from sediment that washed down from the Rocky Mountains, which was mixed with rubble from glaciers. An acre (0.4 hectare) of tall grass prairie contains as much as 250 tons of **topsoil**. In comparison, forest regions generally contain about 20–50 tons of topsoil per acre.

In the north, the steppe is called a meadow steppe. Biologists have counted seventy-three species of plants in 1 square yard (0.8 square meter). The steppe in the south receives less rainfall than the north, so there are not as many forbs. Different types of feather grasses grow here.

the same throughout the area. More rain falls in the east than in the west. For this reason, Ukraine and adjacent parts of Romania have the richest pastureland in the region.

Subtle Importance

"Grasses are very underrated plants," says Charon Geigle, a biologist with the USDA Forest Service at Nebraska National Forest. "Most people don't realize it, but grasses are the most important plants on Earth to human beings." Almost all of our food comes directly or indirectly from grasses. Rice, corn, wheat, barley, oats, rye—all cereal grains—as well as bamboo and sugarcane are all different kinds of grasses. Meat-producing animals either graze on grass on the open range or eat hay on the farm.

From a car window, grasslands may just look like green fields. "I am always in awe of people who drive through a grassland and claim they see nothing," says Geigle. The first pioneers who came through the North American prairies on horseback thought the grasslands were a vast wasteland. Many wrote home about the great desert of grass they had to cross to get to a place where they could live.

"The richness of a grassland is very subtle," says Tim Smith, botanist for the Missouri Department of Conservation. "The Grand Canyon and Rocky Mountains attract a lot of attention because they are impressive even at a distance," he says. "One can drive up to the south rim of the Grand Canyon and immediately see that it is worthy of protection. It takes a little more investigation to find the richness and beauty of a prairie."

This book takes a closer look at that richness.

This subsoil profile shows how much of the grass plant is actually underground. Roots absorb water and minerals from the soil and store food. The vast root system is one of the reasons the grass plant can survive the grassland's harsh environment.

Chapter Two

Tough as Grass

You can step on it, burn it, forget to water it, cover it in ice and snow—and you still won't kill a grass plant. Grasses are tough. The root system, leaves, and method of growing enable these plants to withstand just about anything Mother Nature can conjure.

A grass is a hollow-stemmed plant with narrow leaves and an extensive root system. What we see aboveground is less than half of the plant. Like a tree, most of the grass plant lies under the ground. If they were laid end to end, the roots that anchor just one plant in place would extend for miles. For example, the roots of a single wheat plant would measure more than 40 miles (64 km) if laid end to end.

Roots absorb water and minerals from the soil and store them as food. When there is not much precipitation, roots pull water from the moister layers of soil farther beneath the surface. Even when the aboveground portion of a grass plant is destroyed by drought, fire, or snow, enough energy is stored in the root network to produce new growth.

A Functional Shape

In the grassland, plants are exposed to full sunlight all day. They get sufficient light for **photosynthesis**, the process by which green plants capture energy from the sun and use it to combine carbon dioxide and water to make their own food. But due to limited rainfall, plants here struggle for water.

Cows have four-chamber stomachs because grasses are difficult to digest. Lightly chewed food goes into the first two chambers, and then it is regurgitated to be chewed again. After this pulp or cud goes into the third and fourth chambers for final digestion.

The narrow grass leaf helps keep the plant alive in dry conditions by helping to prevent water loss. Water evaporates from the surface of leaves through a process called **transpiration**. A narrow leaf has less surface area than a wide one. Therefore, less water is lost. Many times, plants will even fold over or close upon themselves to prevent water loss.

Way to Grow

The major growing section of grass—the **basal meristem**, where new plant tissue is produced—is located where the roots and stem meet. This juncture can be either at or below the ground surface. If the plant's leaves are destroyed by fire or trampling, for example, the growing point remains unaffected and the plant will simply grow back.

In contrast, a tree's growing points are located at the tips of the branches. Some trees are killed when these spots are burned. The heat of fire may also affect a tree if it is hot enough to kill the cambium layer, the narrow band of tissue inside the inner bark, which carries food from the leaves to the roots. The tree then dies of starvation.

Types of Grasses

Grasses can be broken into two types: annuals and perennials. Annuals, like wheat, rice, and corn, exist as a seed, grow, produce seed, and die all in the same growing season. Most grassland grasses and those in most lawns are perennials, plants that exist over multiple growing seasons. Although the top of the

Blowing in the Wind

In the grassland, there are so few obstacles to air movement that the wind seems to blow constantly. This accelerates the water evaporation process. This is another reason why narrow leaves are a benefit to grasses.

plant appears dead in winter, a perennial plant's roots live on, sprouting new leaves every year for sometimes as long as fifty years.

Dead leaves and stems from all grasses form a brown mat of vegetation called **litter**, which protects the soil and prevents erosion (the loss of topsoil due to the wind and weather).

Not Flashy

Although you may never see a grass flower, all grasses produce flowers. They are not bright or colorful because grasses don't have to attract insects to ensure pollination. Instead, wind blows the pollen from one grass plant to another. The wind also helps disperse the seeds. In many grasses, the seeds have one to three long, hairlike extensions called awns. These awns cling to the hair of wildlife or livestock or to clothing, helping the grasses travel beyond the parent plant.

Some species do not reproduce through seeds. Instead, they use **vegetative reproduction**, in which a parent plant sprouts new plants through its roots, leaves, or stems.

Don't Forget to Smell the Flowers

Non-woody, flowering plants unrelated to grasses are called **forbs.** These wildflowers bloom on grasslands from early spring until late fall. Grasses may make up about 90 percent of the plants on grassland, but these forbs play extremely important roles in the biome's food chain. Forbs such as lupines and prairie buttercups bud in the spring. Compass plants and

Snow crocuses are the earliest of spring flowers. They often bloom while snow is still on the ground.

The Tallgrass Prairie National Preserve in the Flint Hills of Kansas was created on November 12, 1996.

prairie coneflowers grow during the summer. In the fall, sunflowers and goldenrod bloom. The European and Asian steppe are especially known for their crocuses, tulips, irises, valerians, and hyacinths.

Forbs contain more moisture and nutrients than do grasses. Many forbs store large amounts of food in the form of fruits or large seeds, or in swollen underground roots or stems called tubers. Wildlife depend on these food "warehouses," especially in the winter.

Some of these plants are used for medicine. American Indians from the Omaha Nation used milkweed root to make a salve for wounds. The European settlers used the same root to treat respiratory ailments.

Legumes, members of the pea family, are forbs that are particularly important to grasslands. Clover, soybeans, lentils, and peas are legumes. Bacteria live in the roots of legumes and convert nitrogen in the air into nitrogen compounds that are useful to plants. In return, legumes supply the bacteria with a source of carbon produced by photosynthesis. This enables many legumes to survive in nitrogen-poor conditions. The relationship is a symbiotic one, meaning that two organisms live in close association with each other. Symbiotic relationships can either be beneficial or harmful to either member. In this case, the relationship benefits not only the legume but the

Pass the Legumes, Please

Legumes are the second-largest food crop in the world (cereal grasses are first). The seeds of legumes are rich in high-quality protein, providing people with a highly nutritional food resource.

Soybeans are the only beans that contain the same proteins as meat. Originally grown in the Far East, soybeans were introduced to the United States in the early 1800s. Cooked soybeans can be substituted for diced meat in recipes.

plant community in general because legumes add nitrogen to the soil. Some legumes, such as clover, are a great food source for animals that graze. Others, such as the Lambert crazyweed, can cause erratic behavior and death when eaten by livestock.

A Woody Exception

There is one woody plant that has adapted to grassland life—the ombu of the South American pampa. This evergreen shrub can grow as high as 60 feet (18 meters) and as wide as 50 feet (15 m). To protect itself from fire, the ombu has a massive, fire-resistant trunk that contains water-storage tissue. The shrub also has an enlarged base where water is stored. Cattle don't eat it because the sap is poisonous. The plant is also immune to locusts and other pests. Despite its adaptation, the ombu only dots the pampa due to the area's limited rainfall.

The ombu is called the "lighthouse" of the pampa. People traveling through the grasslands, such as gauchos, value the tree for its shade. Locals brew its leaves to make a hot drink.

Richard Peach poses with his bison on his farm in Wisconsin. Early French settlers correctly called these animals bison. Later an English naturalist described them as "buffalo." Although this name stuck, it is biologically incorrect. "Buffalo" better applies to wild oxen found in Asia and Africa.

Chapter Three

Grazers Big and Small

Richard Peach laughs as he watches his 6-foot (2-m) -tall bison, Big Ugly, roll around in the dirt to keep insects from biting. "It is amazing to watch this 1-ton animal roll like a dog," he says.

When Big Ugly gets up, he leaves quite an impression. The plants beneath him are dug up and the hole he has made is about 20 feet (6 m) in diameter and 10 inches (25 cm) deep. Wallowing, the act of rolling around in the mud like this, helps the environment as well as the bison. The hole left behind fills with water and allows short-lived aquatic organisms, such as algae and mosquito larvae, to grow. When the water dries up, annual grasses and other flowering plants find a place to take root.

Peach raises thirty head of bison on his 100-acre (40-ha) ranch in Monroe, Wisconsin. But this is nothing compared to the giant herds that dominated the Great Plains hundreds of years ago. At one time, more than thirty million bison roamed the Great Plains, forming the biggest mass of large mammals ever to tread the globe.

The bison cleared away old growth while feeding. Their sharp hooves broke up the sod, helping till the soil. Their massive droppings were an excellent source of nutrients for the growing plants.

As American settlers moved westward, the bison were hunted almost to extinction. William F. Cody killed so many in order to supply meat to railroad construction crews that he was nicknamed "Buffalo Bill." The U.S. government recognized that the fates of the bison and the Indians of the Plains were so closely linked that the government encouraged the slaughter of the bison as a means of controlling, if not eradicating, the Indians. Today, there are only a few thousand bison, most of which live in parks, in wildlife refuges, or on ranches like Peach's.

Let Me Introduce . . .

Large animals that graze on the steppe include yaks, sheep, antelopes, gazelles, and camels. One of the most interesting is

Get a Move On

The Plains Indians depended on the bison for food, clothing, and shelter. Because they followed the bison's migration or movement throughout the West, the Plains Indians needed a shelter that could be quickly put together and taken down. The Plains Indians developed the tepee—made by leaning long poles together and covering them with buffalo hide.

the Przewalski horse, which some biologists believe is a direct ancestor of the modern domesticated horse. Pictures of this horse even appear in prehistoric cave paintings.

After the Second World War, the number of Przewalski horses living in the wild quickly declined. The last wild Przewalski horse was sighted in 1969 in Mongolia. In 1977, the Foundation for the Preservation and Protection of the Przewalski Horse was founded, and massive efforts were made to reintroduce the horse into the wild.

Sixteen Przewalski horses were released on a 24,000-acre (9,600-ha) preserve in Mongolia. Today, an increasing number of Przewalski horses run wild on the preserve.

This reintroduction benefited not only the breed of horse but the steppe as well. People realized that in order for the

The Przewalski horse was named after the Russian explorer Nikolai Mikhaylovich Przewalski, who discovered the animal in western Mongolia in the late 1870s.

Przewalski to survive, its **habitat** must be preserved. So the government of Mongolia turned the Hustain Nuruu Preserve into a national park and made the Przewalski horse the country's national symbol.

Let's Do It Again

Biologists are hoping similar efforts will save the pampas deer. This small, reddish-brown South American grazer is in danger of extinction. As of 1993, there were only 1,300 wild pampas deer scattered in isolated locations throughout Argentina and Uruguay. There were about 24,000 in Brazil.

The problem with populations becoming so small, especially when animals are isolated from other family groups, is that they begin to inbreed (mate with family members). Inbreeding weakens the gene pool, increasing the rate of infertility, mutations, and birth defects in the animals. Efforts are now underway to reintroduce the pampas deer to its native range in the hopes of boosting the population and strengthening the gene pool.

Small but Mighty

Small, plant-eating mammals also play important roles in the grasslands. Prairie dogs and their burrowing relatives are the stars of this biome.

Prairie dogs dig miles of interconnected tunnels and dens underground, where they live and raise their young. Up to one

That's a Lot of Dogs

The largest prairie dog colony on record was found in Texas. It contained an estimated 400 million prairie dogs.

thousand animals may live together in these "towns" that range in size from 1 to 1,000 acres (0.4 to 400 ha).

"Prairie dogs are considered a linchpin species of the prairies," says Charon Geigle, a biologist with the Nebraska National Forest. A linchpin species is a plant or animal that is central to the healthy functioning of that ecosystem.

Animals such as badgers, ferrets, hawks, and golden eagles depend on prairie dogs for food. Salamanders, burrowing owls, and black-footed ferrets use prairie dog tunnels for shelter. The prairie dog's digging also helps aerate, or supply air to, the soil. This stimulates plant growth, which in turn, provides more food for grazers.

More than one hundred different types of birds, mammals, plants, and insects depend on these members of the squirrel

A mound marks the entrance to a prairie dog burrow. The mound prevents rainwater from flooding the tunnel and also serves as a lookout station for potential danger. It can range in size from 3 to 10 feet (90 cm to 3 m) in diameter and 6 to 12 inches (15 to 30 cm) high.

family. That is quite a role to play for an animal that stands less than 1 foot tall (30 cm) and weighs anywhere from 1 1/2 to 3 pounds (680 grams to 1.3 kilograms)!

Not all grassland inhabitants have considered prairie dogs to be good neighbors, however. Early settlers had no idea how many benefits the prairie dogs provided the grasslands. In the farmers' minds, these rodents were pests that fed on the grasses needed by livestock. In reality, prairie dogs have a very different diet than do livestock. Because of this unfounded fear, farmers shot, poisoned, or gassed thousands upon thousands of these animals.

In 1919, E.W. Nelson, chief of the Bureau of Biological Survey, estimated that prairie dogs inhabited about 100 million acres (40 million ha) in the United States. But because of these mass slaughters, as well as loss of habitat due to farming activities, three of the five prairie dog species native to the United States are either endangered or threatened.

Cousins

The bobak, or steppe marmot, is roughly the same size as the prairie dog. And like the prairie dog, this ground squirrel lives in an underground colony and manages the vegetation around it. An adult bobak eats up to 3 pounds (1.5 kg) of food a day and obtains all the water it needs from its food. These animals are much less social than prairie dogs, rarely interacting with others outside their own families.

The pampa version of the prairie dog is the viscacha, a

scrubland-dwelling rodent of the chinchilla family. It grows up to be 2 feet (61 cm) long with an 8 inch (20 cm) tail, and weighs 15 pounds (7 kg). Viscachas live in colonies of up to thirty individuals. They usually feed at night on grasses, roots, and seeds.

Mini but Mighty

Although mammals may be the most noticeable wildlife on the grassland, insects outnumber and consume far more grasses and other plants than all the mammals and birds put together.

Just in the tallgrass prairie region of North America, there are 100 different species of ants and more than 150 species of bees. Insects help build soil by recycling nutrients. Many insects eat leaves, plant sap, nectar, other insects, and dead animals. Nutrients stored in these items are returned to the

Marmots are true hibernators, meaning that during the long winter, they slow their rate of breathing and their body temperature will drop almost to the freezing point. Their body temperature does not stay down all winter, however. They wake periodically and then go back into deep hibernation.

soil through the insect's scat, or waste. Insects also serve as a major food source for birds and other animals.

Insects also help forbs reproduce by assisting in pollination. Sphinx moths pollinate orchids, and digger bees pollinate milkweed, for example. Botanist Tim Smith from the Missouri Department of Conservation is finding that some forbs are actually dying out because there aren't enough bees to pollinate them. "This is mainly due to the fact that there isn't enough land to support the pollinators," he says.

Farmers divide the prairies in order to plant their crops. A field of corn might be separated from another field by an acre (0.4 ha) of unplowed land. This practice means that there are only fragments or small parcels of prairies where forbs can grow. This discourages pollinators, such as sphinx moths, which often have to travel long distances between fragments. If there are not enough orchids in a fragment for sphinx moths to pollinate, the sphinx moths will stop visiting that area. If the orchid is not pollinated, it is unable to reproduce. The orchid will eventually disappear from that fragment as the individual plant dies.

What's for Dinner?

In certain parts of the world, grasshoppers are eaten as food—dried, jellied, roasted, dipped in honey, or ground into a meal.

Hop Hop

Perhaps the most visible insect on the grassland is the grasshopper. Grasshoppers are everywhere. This is good news for the birds and reptiles that eat grasshoppers. These high-jumping insects can grow to be up to 4 inches (10 cm) in length. They smell through their antennae and hear by means of a **tympanic organ**, a pressure-sensing organ for sound reception located at the base of the abdomen.

There are more than four hundred known species of grasshoppers just in the western United States. While most of these are helpful, about two dozen species are considered to be pests. For example, locusts, a type of migrating grasshopper, are particularly harmful when they multiply out of control. The sky turns black as billions of insects fill the air, searching for food. They devour every green plant in their path. Eventually, the swarms die out because of a lack of food, a change of climate, or an increase in predators.

Grasshoppers have two pairs of wings. The front pair is leathery and narrow. The hind wings are membranous and fan-shaped.

Saker falcons live on open plains and forest steppes in Mongolia, southern Siberia, and the Russian Altai Mountains. Falconers (people who train hawks for hunting) in Arab countries often trap young birds as they migrate to the Middle East.

Chapter Four

Predators Feathery, Furry, and Slippery

The brown steppe saker falcon dives at the weasel at 200 miles (320 km) per hour. The bird catches the weasel in its claws. The weasel screams as it tries to claw its attacker, but the falcon's hold is sure. Soon, the fight is over.

Dozens of species of birds live more or less exclusively on grasslands. All are predators, eating insects or small mammals. Grassland birds may supplement their diet with grass and flower seeds, but because of the weather, these are not always available.

With no trees, birds either fasten their nests to a cluster of grass stems or build them on the ground. Meadowlarks weave grass stalks together to form a dome over the nest to protect the eggs from the burning sun.

Birds that nest on the ground are much more vulnerable to predators than are tree-nesting birds. Ground nests are in danger of being raided by snakes, weasels, or foxes that eat eggs and young birds. To compensate, grassland birds

Meadowlarks are members of the blackbird family. They eat insects in the sumer and seeds during the fall and winter months.

sport brown and white striped feathers, which are a perfect camouflage when the birds are sitting on eggs. They nest and live in areas that match their feathers and coloring so perfectly that they seem to disappear completely from sight. One can be standing right on top of a bird and not see it until it moves.

For added protection, many grassland birds travel in flocks. It is difficult for predators to approach a large group of birds without being seen. Prairie chickens, several species of black-

More Land, Please

"Grassland birds are undergoing a serious decline," says John Pearson, plant ecologist for the Iowa Department of Natural Resources. Grassland fowl require large pieces of land on which to complete their life cycles. Due to farming activities, there are only fragments of prairie land available. Many birds are failing to reproduce in these smaller areas. One reason is that they cannot find nesting sites. Those that do lay eggs find that their nests are not well hidden from predators. Twenty nests in a smaller area are much easier to find than twenty nests in a larger area. This means there are fewer nests that will go undetected by predators.

Ostriches live only in Africa. Females lay the largest eggs in the world. One ostrich egg can weigh up to 3 pounds (1.3 kg) and measure 6 inches (15 cm) in length and 5 inches (12.5 cm) in diameter.

birds, horned larks, cowbirds, goldfinches, longspurs, and sandhill cranes form flocks not only during their migration but also throughout the year.

The ostrich is the largest bird in both the grassland community and the world. A male may stand more than 9 feet (2.7 m) tall and weigh almost 700 pounds (318 kg). Although the bird can't fly, it can run on its long legs, reaching speeds of 44 miles (71 km) per hour.

An ostrich look-alike, the American rhea, lives on the pampa of South America. The rhea is also a flightless bird with long legs and a long neck. It can weigh up to 51 pounds (23 kg). Rheas are omnivorous, meaning they eat plants,

seeds, roots, fruit, insects, and small vertebrates. In this species, the male is the predominant caregiver. He will mate with up to twelve females. Afterward, he builds a nest in which each female lays her eggs. The male incubates anywhere from ten to sixty eggs at once.

Furry

At one time, wolves were common on grasslands in North America, Europe, and Asia. But people so feared these animals that they've been hunted and killed throughout history. Between the excess hunting and the loss of their habitat due to farming, these animals, including the South American pampa jaguar, have moved to forest communities. Today, the primary predators of the grasslands are smaller animals.

The rhea resembles the ostrich but is not related. Scientists believe this similarity is due to convergent evolution—when different species develop similar physical characteristics because they have had to adapt to similar environmental conditions.

The kit fox, the badger, and the ferret are predators that are perfectly adapted for North American prairie life. The kit fox of the short-grass prairie has large ears that radiate heat to help the animal deal with the hot summer temperatures. The fox's extra long legs help it run fast so it can catch jackrabbits and pounce on prairie dogs before they reach their tunnels.

Badgers are best known for their claws. They are well equipped for digging and like to dine on small burrowing animals, such as prairie dogs. The black-footed ferret, a member

of the weasel family, also feeds on prairie dogs and uses the dogs' burrows for its dens. The decline in the prairie dog population has seriously affected the ferret population as well. Some biologists fear that the black-footed ferret may be headed for extinction.

Kit foxes are the second smallest dog in the world. They feed mainly at night and rely on speed and nearness to their dens for safety.

The American badger is such a powerful digger that it can easily outdistance a man with a shovel. When cornered, the badger can be a fierce fighter.

The Cat of South America

The Geoffroy's cat may be the most abundant small cat in the pampa. Its silver-gray coat is spotted with black. The Geoffroy's cat has adapted to human presence better than many other cat species in South America. While most animals fear man and will flee from disturbed areas, the Geoffroy's cat seeks them out, taking advantage of the lack of competition for food from other predators. The animal is easily trapped and tamed. Some South Americans keep the cat as a pet, while others consider it good eating.

Slippery

Amphibians require an aquatic habitat for at least part of their life cycle, so they are scarce in the grassland ecosystem. The *Xenopus* (meaning "strange foot") or clawed frog of the veldt is one exception. This small, pond-dwelling frog has long, unwebbed fingers and no tongue. It uses its fingers to fan food

Clawed frogs evolved 125 million years ago, when dinosaurs still roamed the planet.

toward the mouth. Typically, clawed frogs never leave the water. However, they will migrate if their pond dries up.

Another exception is the largest land-dwelling salamander in the world, the tiger salamander, which calls the North American prairies home. Larger salamanders will eat animals as large as mice. Tiger salamanders breed in early spring when the rains arrive. During the dry weather, they spend most of their time underground, often in abandoned prairie dog burrows.

Reptiles do not require as much water as amphibians do, and several species are found in grasslands. The prairie rattlesnake can grow to be anywhere from 35 to 45 inches (90 to 115 cm) long. Its diamond-shaped head is set off from its relatively thin neck. Harmless snakes with similar coloring will imitate the rattlesnake's warning signal. One can tell them apart by looking at the end of the tail. When a prairie rattlesnake rattles, it holds its tail high off the ground. A harmless snake will vibrate its tail to make a similar sound, but the tail must be held close to the ground to produce noise because it has no rattles in its tail.

Tiger salamanders resist periods of drought by hiding belowground. They are listed as endangered primary because of loss of habitat.

A female biologist keeps a watchful eye on this controlled burn, making sure that the flames do not cross the fire break.

Chapter Five

Giving Mother Nature a Hand

John Pearson, dressed in yellow protective clothing, drips liquid fire from what looks like a large torch onto the prairie land. The flames feed on the dry grasses like a starved animal, and the wind gives the blaze feet, carrying it higher and deeper into the prairie grasses.

"I started the backfire," he says into a walkie talkie. "We're ready," answers Kevin Pape, a park ranger, from the other side of the prairie.

Suddenly, a gust of wind blowing in the wrong direction sends flames toward Pearson, igniting the grasses beside him. A woman also dressed in yellow rushes to smother the flames with a large rubber flap attached to a long handle.

"Thanks, Mary," says Pearson, a plant ecologist with the Iowa Department of Natural Resources.

These biologists are purposely setting fire to 30 acres (12 ha) of prairie in Stone State Park in northwestern Iowa. "We call this a prescribed burn," says Pearson.

Useful Flames

Before human settlers arrived, fires burned across the prairies on a regular basis. Lightning often sparked blazes. Plains Indians also started fires to attract game to the new grasses that flourish after a fire has occurred.

Fire serves two purposes. First, the flames keep woody vegetation, such as trees and shrubs, from growing. Second, fires help recycle nutrients back into the ground.

"It is so dry out here that nothing decomposes [breaks down]," says Charon Geigle. Dead leaves, stems, and flowers accumulate year after year. The litter traps valuable nutrients needed for other plants to grow. Fire decomposes the dead vegetation instantly, allowing the stored nutrients to return to the soil in the form of ash.

"The frequency of prairie fires today is almost zero," says Pearson, due to the fact that people suppress fires. Not only has this allowed a plethora of trees and shrubs to take root but

the soil also isn't being replenished. Biologists purposely set fire to prairies to match their historical frequency—about once every four years in tallgrass prairie.

Other Tools

Biologists also use livestock grazing as a tool to maintain the prairie, says Geigle. Livestock such as cattle and sheep are the "large grazers" of today's grasslands, serving a similar function as the American bison. Cows eat a certain portion of the dead plants and return nutrients to the ground through their droppings. The hoof action of livestock helps "plant" seeds and till the soil.

Biologists don't burn an entire prairie at once because small animals and insects that live in dead litter on the ground have no place to go if the entire prairie is burned. Instead, biologists divide the area into sections and burn a different section each year.

If left to graze in one area too long, however, livestock can kill the grass and forbs, which is what has happened to much of the prairie. The area's natural grazers, bison and pronghorn, migrated through the Great Plains. They grazed part of the prairie and then moved on, allowing the eaten areas to regrow. The original settlers, however, erected fences and let their cattle fend for themselves. Cattle were moved to greener pastures only once an area was totally stripped of grasses. With no native vegetation left, the topsoil often dried out and blew away. Today, people understand the need to rotate livestock between fields.

An Unwelcome Visitor

"The biggest problem facing prairies today is the introduction of non-native plants," says Pearson. "These plants do not normally grow in an area but have been introduced to the environment through human intervention."

Such an unwanted guest is leafy spurge, a plant that typically grows in the steppes of Asia. It was imported to the United States around 1897. When it arrived, the plant found a great habitat but no natural enemies. The spurge spread like wildfire over the Great Plains. Leafy spurge chokes out native plants. For the past one hundred years, it has been converting native prairies into acres of just leafy spurge, rendering the land less useful or attractive to natural prairie plants or animals.

To find a solution to this overgrowth, scientists went to Asia and studied insect species that hold leafy spurge in check. They decided to release the leafy spurge beetle in the United States after ensuring that the insect would not be a problem for native prairie plants and animals. Early results are promising. "In just the few years we've been using these beetles, they seem to be setting back the leafy spurge growth," says Pearson.

Of the 400,000 square miles (1,036,000 sq km) of tallgrass prairie that once covered the North American continent, less than 4 percent remains.

Chapter Six

In Your Hands

One of the major environmental concerns regarding temperate grasslands is the conversion of grassland to farms. Because the rich soil is so ideal for farming and grazing, many natural grasslands have already been lost. Instead of native grass plants, grasslands now support corn, wheat, and other grains. They also provide grazing areas for sheep and cattle. Although the food supplied by these farmlands is important, so are the plants and animals that live in this unique biome.

Dust in the Wind

Desertification is not a new concept. In the 1930s, the Great Plains were turned into a desert when the region suffered a seven-year drought. Due to poor farming practices and overcultivation, there was no native vegetation to hold the topsoil in place. Winds carried the soil away. "Black blizzards" of windblown soil blocked out the sun and piled the dirt into great dunes. Dust storms swept all the way to Washington, D.C., where President Franklin D. Roosevelt had to wipe dust from his desk constantly. Thousands of farmers went bankrupt. Eventually, with federal aid, people erected windbreaks and restored much of the grass. By the 1940s, the area had recovered.

A Warm Threat

Grasslands are also threatened by global warming. Global warming theory predicts that the rapid increase in the concentration of greenhouse gases in our atmosphere due to human activities will warm Earth at a rate that is faster than at any time in human history. This warming will affect the amount of precipitation Earth receives.

Grasslands already hang in a precarious balance regarding their need for rainfall. Any more or less will destroy this biome and its wildlife. One possible scenario of global warming is that higher temperatures would increase the rate at which water evaporates from the soil. If the amount that evaporates every year is greater than the amount that falls, the soil would become drier, and the grassland would change into desert.

Worldwide **desertification** already threatens an estimated 40 percent of the world's land surface. This desertification is caused by erosion—when topsoil blows off the surface of the land because there is no vegetation to hold it in place.

Each year, desertification converts more than 55,000 square miles (88,500 sq km) of land into desert, causing billions of dollars in damage and displacing countless thousands of people.

Why Bother?

There are many reasons why these grasslands should be preserved. First, they are as much a part of a country's heritage as any national monument. Second, if the native grasslands are destroyed, wildlife that can live only in this type of environment will go extinct because of human activity. Not only do some people believe this is ethically wrong, but scientists don't know what impact this might have on the rest of the world and other biomes. Third, grasses and forbs have the capacity to absorb carbon dioxide. This helps slow global warming.

Finally, many of our medicines are produced from plants. Dr. Wayne Morton, president of the Missouri Prairie Foundation, estimates that 80 percent of the microorganisms that live solely on the prairie have yet to be identified. Within these unidentified microorganisms lies a tremendous potential for new medications.

Solutions

Efforts to restore and preserve grasslands are going on all over the world. In Europe and Asia, areas of steppe that were plowed during an attempted agricultural expansion in the 1950s have been allowed to revert to their natural state. In Russia, many areas that have never been plowed have been

"We can preserve native grassland and still have enough land for farming if we make sensible agricultural and environmental choices," says John Pearson.

turned into nature preserves, ensuring that they never will be developed. The remainder of the natural veldt in Africa is now in the Great Limpopo Transfrontier Park.

In North America, organizations such as the Nature Conservancy, the Iowa Department of Natural Resources, and the Missouri Prairie Foundation buy unspoiled grasslands and set them aside as nature preserves. "But finding prairie fragments that have escaped being destroyed or cultivated is like finding a piece of gold," says Pearson. Untouched prairie is rare and valuable. Such areas are small—usually less than 40 acres (16 ha) and often less than 1 acre (0.4 ha). No matter what size the prairies are, though, the organizations mentioned still want them. "We can't be too choosy anymore," says Pearson. "We don't have room to lose any more grasslands."

Conservation organizations also buy abandoned farms or areas on existing farms that owners do not wish to develop. These groups then turn that land back into prairie.

"We are handicapped in that we need to find the seeds of plants that originally grew here," says Pearson. "It is difficult to find the kind of seeds we need in the volume we need."

Restoration is an intricate practice. "It took Mother Nature ten thousand years to develop the prairie, and people destroyed it in less than one hundred years," says Smith. "It will be a number of lifetimes before we can hope to get it back to something resembling an undisturbed prairie." And even then, some of the things that made a grassland a grassland, such as many of the large grazers, are gone for good.

You Bring Hope

There is good news. Agricultural improvements allow farmers to produce more food on smaller plots of land. Today, many areas not needed for growing food are being allowed to revert back to native grasses.

As more people put more effort into saving grasslands, someone in the future—maybe you—will come up with better ways to preserve what now exists. And then maybe the Prairie Chicken Bed & Breakfast can once again open its doors.

Glossary

basal meristem—growing point of a grass where new plant tissue is produced

biome—community of living organisms within an ecological region defined by climate

desertification—the conversion of productive land to a desertlike condition by overgrazing or other removal of the protective vegetation that prevents erosion

forb—broad-leafed flowering, herbaceous plant that is not grasslike

habitat—food, water, shelter, and space needed for wildlife to survive

legume—member of the pea family

litter—dead vegetation that makes up the uppermost layer of soil

photosynthesis—process by which green plants capture energy from the sun and use it to combine carbon dioxide and water to make their own food

sod—dense mat of grass roots that protect the soil from water and wind erosion

topsoil—layer of earth in which minerals and other nutrients are available for plant growth

transpiration—evaporation of water from aboveground plant parts. It occurs primarily at the leaves while their pores are open to allow the passage of carbon dioxide and oxygen during photosynthesis

tympanic organ—organ for sound reception found in moths, grasshoppers, and one variety of cicada

vegetative reproduction—form of reproduction in which plants reproduce by means of roots, leaves, or stems rather than with seeds

To Find Out More

Books for Further Reference

Behar, Susie. *Closer Look at Grasslands*. Brookfield, Conn.: Copper Beech Books, 2000.

Patent, Dorothy Hinshaw. *Life in a Grassland*. Minneapolis: Lerner Publications Company, 2003.

Rotter, Charles. *An Enduring Spirit: The Prairie*. Mankato, Minn.: Creative Education, 2002.

Scheff, Duncan. *Grasslands*. New York: Raintree Steck-Vaughn Publishers, 2001.

Stein, Paul. *Biomes of the Future*. New York: Rosen Publishing Group, Inc., 2001.

Organizations and Online Sites

Blue Planet Biomes
www.blueplanetbiomes.org

The World's Biomes
www.ucmp.berkeley.edu/glossary/gloss5/biome

Global 200: Blueprint for a Living Planet
www.panda.org/about_wwf/where_we_work/ecoregions/global200/pages/home.htm

Missouri Prairie Foundation
P.O. Box 200
Columbia, MO 65205
www.moprairie.org
Founded in 1966, the Missouri Prairie Foundation is a land conservancy that uses donations to purchase and preserve prairie tracts. It is also an educational organization.

The Nature Conservancy
4245 North Fairfax Drive, Suite 100
Arlington, VA 22203-1606
http://nature.org

National Grasslands Visitor Center
708 Main Street, PO Box 425

Wall, SD 57790
Telephone: 605-279-2125
www.fs.fed.us/r2/nebraska/units/frrd/ngvisitor.html

Tallgrass Prairie National Preserve
PO Box 585, 226 Broadway
Cottonwood Falls, KS 66845
Telephone: 620-273-6034
Fax: 620-273-6099
www.nps.gov/tapr/home.htm

A Note on Sources

I start every project by scanning the Internet and visiting the library to get background information. There are a surprising number of good, recent books on the grasslands, such as *Life in a Grassland* by Dorothy Hinshaw Patent. This indicates to me that awareness of this special biome is certainly growing.

My favorite way to find out about an area is to talk to the people who live and work there. This not only helps to verify the information, but also gives the story life. In this case, I contacted Charon Geigle from the USDA Forest Service; Elaine Kaelke of the Prairie Chicken Bed & Breakfast; Richard Peach, owner of Monti Bison Ranch in Monroe, Wisconsin; John Pearson from the Iowa Department of Natural Resources; and Tim Smith from the Missouri Department of Conservation. I also contacted the National Grasslands Visitor Center and the Missouri Prairie Foundation. All of these dedicated people are

59

passionately concerned about the grasslands they work to conserve. I also drew upon my own experience of living in the Midwest as an employee of the Missouri Department of Conservation. Newspaper and magazine articles rounded out my research.

—*Laurie Peach Toupin*

Index

Numbers in *italics* indicate illustrations.

About the Author

Laurie Peach Toupin visited the prairies often when she worked for the Missouri Department of Conservation. She loved the openness of the grassland, where one can see a storm coming from miles away.

Laurie left a career as an environmental engineer to become a journalist. Today, she is a freelance writer who writes articles and books about science and nature for publications such as *Odyssey*, a science magazine for children, and *The Christian Science Monitor*.

She lives in Pepperell, Massachusetts with her daughters, her husband, two dogs, and a cat. When she first moved to New England, she often felt hemmed in because of all the trees and houses. Although she appreciates New England's tall pines and lush rivers and streams, she misses the beauty and calm of the prairie.